Moonscapes

Light and Dark

Jeremy Langrish

Horsa Editions 2014

Fist edition Horsa Editions 2006

Second edition. Prepared for print by Horsa Editions 2014

Printed at www.Lulu.com

Horsa Editions
3 St Lukes Rd.,
Maidstone
Me145AR

For Maggie Harris

Thank you for 'directing' me from Peckam Library
to the Brown Jug, after which I began to find my
voice.

Maggie

You are a Guyanan Woman
and the Rhythm
flows in your blood.
Feet tapping beat and your voice
rising, falling
in strict measure
as you look around
as you read.
See how your words
have me under your spell.

And for Martin Holdsworth, who said that the moon
was much neglected in Poetry. Here you are.

Contents

No Fixed Abode

There was a road with a sign *six fish fly only*
that lead to a lazy river.
But on the way

there was a house that had no address
no letter-box and where
no postmen called.

There were the sounds that monkeys make
in the wild beyond the garden
in afternoons.

There was a fly-screen of fine wire mesh
sensuous to fingernail before the front door under
the acacia tree,

there were red concrete floors and too few mats
and dogs that scraped and slipped with
boisterous greetings.

There were visitors that came unannounced
and cooking smells and china cups
and rich orange tea.

Last Chance

Auschwitz: 60 years on 27th Jan 2005 BRZEZINKA, POLAND.
Broadcast BBC2, afternoon. Auschwitz. 60 years after
liberation. Survivors of the holocaust, Jew, Roma, Sinti, meet
and remember the death camp. 1.5 million people
exterminated here over 3 years. They tell us again and we
hear.

I

On snow, under snow
We return to tell again
(Lord one blessing: the world hear us now)
As though for the first time
As though for the last time
We remember our peoples

With us, our guests, elderly men
And women. Leaders of men,
Of Churches, of Nations
Men with sonorous voices,
With Passion, with eloquence.

In this cemetery there are no graves, no stones
The ashes of our peoples
Trodden into Europe's soil
Our blood in the rivers
This place of madness
Of Pain, of Death,
Its victims our community
Remembered by us, remembered for you
In pain, in images
Too horrific to see, too vile to speak.

There was nothing normal here. Just:
Trains full on arrival
Empty on leaving
And extermination, cremation.
Or if not extermination
Starving, beating, labour
Then extermination
Concealed from the world. Pain:
Of partings, of dyings – too painful to live.
Too absurd, too painful to die.

Stand still for our memories.
We were children then,
We lived, now we return together.
Let us remember our families
Blow the shofar
Say Kaddish for us. Pray.

II

Let me remember shame
My father's shame
My father's father's shame
In the madness, the unbelieving
Of what is not for believing

The madness of a fascist future
Deliberate, dispassionate
Uncompromising
To remove your humanity
Your dignity
Your memory

All traces of your races.
The ashes of your peoples
Be trodden into Europe's soil
Your blood in the rivers.

When you called out
We did not hear
And you return.

Today you honour your liberators
Your leaders honour you
We honour you

We, obliged by your imperative
That this dismal, eerie place
– Where we hear your countrymen
Cry out beneath our feet –
Be fixed in our hearts:
For remembrance

Of madness
Of inhumanity
Of power.
To know man's darkest nature
And never forget.

And pray for your peace
Till the end of your days.

Sprung Colour

Against a blue sky divesting its grey
encumbrance, slender is the birch. Silver
its bark, and branches delicately sprigged,
and buds that urge the smallest pale green leaves,
and yellow catkins hang, sway so lightly
in a warming breeze, silent chimes of spring.

Waiting

This is morning, already
woken before me. I step
out step into the dazzle
of the East, and long shadows –
mine glued to my feet.
I follow it, follow in and out
of shade, warm and cool
and I turn at the end of the street
back into the dazzle –
I look up. pigeons, gulls
cross the sky before cloud,
the sun still rising and shadows shorten.

And I know that if they had come early
it could have been a good day for the swifts.

Promises

When your hair was still brown about your shoulders
we played house, made babies and promises.
Sometimes you wore silver in your ears,

but

The sun's trudges from dawn to dusk are flashes
swept by time into memory's crevices.
We mark days to remember promises
made and kept, and babies grown and flown.
Suddenly you say *it's Silver*. We buy silver

but

the silver in your hair flashing in sun
is a gift and a kindness of Time
to one still sworn after so many years.

Crow

Brat-pack flat-cap crow alone in the tree,
Sky rat sneaking some space over my patch,
Dominating, and looking down on me
So I know brilliant darkness, and Big.
Sharp its eye – I half expected a wink.
It raised its wings like a bat, beak ajar
In silent disdain. Its words could have said
Yeah right! **You** *walk the talk of the Sacred Law,*
Flicker between the shining and the lit
Flutter between the shadows and the shade
Range between yesterdays and tomorrows
Ride on the shuttle of destiny's loom!
I so humbled. It heaved into the sky
Allowing me just enough time to say
'Morning, my Lord! before its first wings' flap.

Broken Daydream

I walked the river by the lock
before the sun was in the sky,
I thought of casting baited hook
to the ripples of the bubbles
and drawing out a silver fish.

On the other side five geese grazed,
and yellow was the rowan's fruit
before the lock-house. On the wall
across the water in the lock
the boatman's ladder rose, its rails
in still dirty green and chill clutch.

But then glamour on the sheen,
Lock-house, ladder, geese and tree
were upside down! I saw the sky,
a seagull swam among the clouds.

One goose flopped into the water
with splash and ripple on the glaze,
the scene was stirring under waves.
I thought of one who upside down
ascend the ladder from below
and if his feet should break the air
might shudder all my world and me.

I heard the gull call overhead,
heard the water in the sluice
and by a grill I saw this world's
detritus gathered in a swirl;
broken leaf and twig and scum
and bottle labelled lemonade.

Swift

Swift

but

stuttering

against

the   blue

weaving   a

dazzle   of

sunlight   into

feathers

under

wings

soar,   flutter,   swoop

as   they   they   and

turn,   as   into

dive   weaving   delight   and   rising   spirit

the

sky,

making

them   sure,

making   them

constant

making

them

swift

Creiddylad

She slips upon the wheel of stars
marking a time longer than the day
ranging the sky according to season
growing, receding light and dark,
birth and death, month on month.

By light, by night beware the moon.
Her love, her wisdom
and deceit makes old souls wise
else foolish, other than themselves.
Bewitched, seduced
with silver that men value,
her light silver bright but at morning
frost or dew or rising mist.

See her fickle as a girl
torn between two lovers.
Upon her face do light and dark,
Life and death, two twins,
enjoin an endless test.
Matched in wile and guile,
one rouses, draws her in,
entices her, then the other
turns her head that she cannot sit still.

See her by the sea,
flowers strewn before her steps –
see the very water rise to greet her flight.

By the Way

Quiet on the river's lazy drift
are two canoes idle on the water,
tired arms that ache, remember their exertion,
tired hands clutch paddle-shafts over decks.
Quiet their breathing in the still air,
David and she are watching the water
glazed with the sky's light behind the trees'
reflections. Fey here, where the lily-pads
gleam and decorate the place, the secret
time seldom seen, where above the lilies
azure darts sweep and soar as
dragonflies have their day.

Take Art

In colours of blood, and sinew, and bone
show me *heart*. Show me loves dreams and chafes,
birth, its pain, and death's dreary frustrations.
Show me pulse: water, red earth and fire
from air, coursing my veins, kindling passion,
show me the beat in living's ebbs and flows.

See the Potter mix a paste with water,
white clay and bone ash, and throw a pot
so delicate, and on it paint the colours
of dawn, of sea, earth, tree and leaf, and night,
and fire it in his kiln to harden, glaze.
When cool it is a very pretty thing.

Earth, water, fire in air – imaginings
on porcelain or in the pulsing heart.

Bound

A kite hung from a string in my hand
light on my fingers but a sadness,
a hung wing drooping as though in mourning,
sideways hanging, depleted.

In the distance a rustle of leaf
and under my hand a flutter
of fabric and wing stretching, rising
in hope, pulling at me.

The string unwinds. Above is exuberance
in sway and hover, and colour
swaggering in the sky, glad to be tugging
at strings in my heart.

Beeing

Beewise

I want to go where the honeybee goes
with a bounce and a buzz and a blur of wing,
to the call of the trumpets that hang
in a shimmer, or flick in a passing breeze.

I want six feet under me where she lands,
where wings fold on her back, and she wades
through tendrils of gender, where seeds are born,
where seminal dust brushes her hair yellow.

I want to drink as the honeybee drinks
where lip curls to a straw to reach
the droplets of sweetness at petals end,
and back, and on, replete.

I want to preen as the honeybee preens
combing the itches, straightening tangle
restoring the cut of her velvet coat
bold in the black, bright in the golden brown.

I want to fly with the bee bloated,
swinging in air, blown with nectar,
and baskets of harvest for honey, for hive
to sisters, to dance, to her Queen

Ask for the Moon

'Jamas on and ready for bed,
moon, she said, *please.* I picked her up.
In crook of arm, on hip she sat,
one hand, one arm on my shoulder.
The garden door, approached and opened,
from the threshold we looked out,
carefully stepped into the dark.
Her other hand, its fist forward,
extended a finger, pointed -
my moon, she said. *In my garner*
and I, delighted by her glee,
was proud to have delivered wishes.

Despondent

Morning sun hidden
behind cool grey. Dull sight,
dull senses today.

Morning: cool grey dims
yesterdays bright vistas – dull,
today diminished.

Elementary

Ever the boundless sky, the depth of ocean,
the incandescence of sun, the weight of continents
made substance by their own will,
forever combining at perception's edge,
charming with skipping and mirth,
or scaring with malice and dance.

Children's stuff – shrill voice in unprepared ear,
and laughter; tinkle of bell, xylophone melody,
clutching at hearts. Glints, glimmers
of flutter of leaf, rain in sunshine
sparks among flame, crystal in cleaved stone
under moonlit wings,

or grown up stuff – reverberant voice that spellbinds,
and fear; bubbling mud, slurp of tongue
gripping viscera. Glance and glimpse
of broken tree, face in cloud,
lightning bolt, scarp of crag
under flap of leather.

Between leaf and tree, crystal and crag,
between remembering and forgetting,
ever the prescience of mirth and malice,
of petal and bile in the mouth
when laughter and fear meet
in moments out of time.

I like people but I couldn't eat a whole one.

Ordinary and everyday is flush of cheek,
trust in passion when lips meet
in promise of delirious excess,
vulnerable and trusting, sharing secrets,
in banter, camaraderie and illusion
understood by each, discounted and dismissed,
and exhilaration in argument, alive in anger.
There's comfort in the mobile 'phone
and baseball bat on car seat when alone.

For some among the people that you meet
you cannot know, you wouldn't understand
a secret that they never tell.
They come alive in others' shock
and their esteem for you as meat
means slaughter, blood and butchery,
filleting and dicing and freezing
and later dishes may be shared
at tables where they guard their secrets zealously.

No Second Chance

The Dark offers no sense,
no shape to feel or eye to catch
no ear to hear
no delight, disgust in nose and mouth.

Here an illusion of space, and other;
place to be and barrier to penetrate,
and a suspicion of sentience
and some vague hankering after,
and offer of rest for the rest of forever.

The Dark is stirred by memories
of incident and sentiment
liken to the pages of a book
or facsimile or residue,
whose aspects re-define
the fractures and the failures of a life
otherwise forgotten.

But even in the drawings of life and love
or if some loved-one incants, invokes, pleads
the restoration of the glue that binds body and mind,
that took a lifetime to grow,
that heals corruption or gathers dissipated elements
from wind and sea,
the glue that restores the tangible, vibrant, delectable
and fractured, failed life
what choices there?

The Moment of Glide

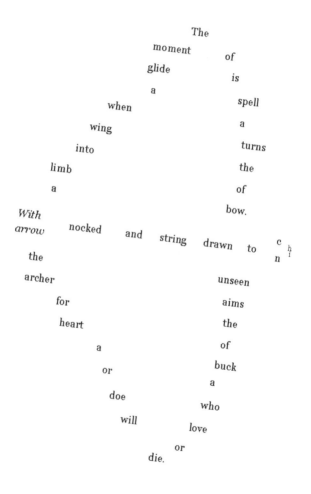

The
moment   of
glide
                 is
    a
 when   spell
  wing   a
   into   turns
  limb   the
   a   of
                 bow.
With
arrow   nocked   and   string   drawn   to   c
                                                n h
 the   i
 archer   unseen
  for   aims
  heart   the
     a   of
      or   buck
                                  a
      doe   who
       will   love
                          or
                    die.

32

Mendacity

What if there is deliberate deceit, or deceit discovered?

Words heard, moulded by a forked tongue,
silk and sleaze, side by side
and eyes' brightness fades.
Sink. Care less.
All the snakes in the world
gathering at door, window, feet,
cool coils wrapped about limb and body,
all sinking beneath the gloom.
Silk to sleaze beneath fang and venom,
and words have faded
behind more pressing sounds:
a slither, slide, slip, a rasp of scale.
There, shudder, and care less.
See momentarily a forked tongue,
as if imagined only, but in that moment,
manifest, the forked tongue flickers.
Care not for venom, fang, or rasp of scale
over cold skin, or cool coil pressing on limb,
care only for the fork in the tongue transfixed.

Warriors in Waiting

Keeping distance, balancing rage with fear
accepting consequence, while in the Dark
what the world does to them shifts the balance.
They stride to the venue, strut about the cage,
blokes. Equal blokes, pretty and mean, reduced
to basics, stripped to the core, taking risk.
Abnegating fear, raging against rage,
smacking the rage, and one exerting blows,
exacting pain, once, again and again.
One victor, one vanquished, and success is
guilty secrets, life choices realised,
and to weep in the darkness at loss, and gain,
rocked by emotion, unknown, or half-known:
a flicker, briefest moment in the Dark.

Something Sacred Shows Itself

Tankerton Beach. Easter Saturday 2007

Before us Nammu ever was, will be the salty sea.
That day, we were there,
Gracie and me.

That day Nammu's waves were gentle, refracting
and reflecting, that she wore the colours
of the pebbles,

and they took on her gloss, and they rattled
in rhythm, inspiring and sighing,
for her breathing.

There, gentle waves slumped and rolled, reaching
with nimble fingers for the pretty things
along the shore,

as did we, with our bucket and bare feet,
the *chuck* of pebble on plastic, the *ack*
of stone on stone

and when the bucket was full, too heavy
for Grace, we took our stones, threw them one by one
to Nammu's grasp –

offerings – she stirred for each one, rippling,
acknowledging, and I knew that in time
she'd return them.

My Name, My Soul

I

What is my name when
From below the ground
The Potter casts me up?
The name of my shade
Sheltered from the tears of the sun?

What is my name when
I see her or a flower of the field
And my heart is light?
Or when body does as bidden
And design wrought?

What is my name when
My image is seen?
And who goes when called?
Who hungers, thirsts, craves
And who takes satisfaction?

Thrust from the ground
To stand between earth and sky
And catch the tears of the sun,
Feet of clay, ground from ground.
In the morning your shade marks my depletion
At midday the tears rain down
At evening I sustain as weary tears dry.

Who but I peeps from the eyes of others
And calls out names?
Where you crave, my craving
Your intentions mine,
Satisfaction is mine.
I know the names...

II

What is my name when
In the dark there are none to see
None to call? At the end of days
Reposed among stars
Or decomposed in the belly of the serpent?

I call out in the dark.
When shadows merge
I sustain.
Daily the Potter moulds you anew
To my design.

At the end of days we tell the scribe
Our name. Our heart,
Weighed against Truth, Justice,
Reassembles, soars to the stars
Or dissembles; we sink below
Returned by worms.

I know our Names...

Philippa

In sun, bright about her hat
and hair light upon her back
slight summer-white dress
loose about her knee
she walked bare legged, spritely
on the grass between the thistles.

Colourful children tended the chestnut
one a girl, one a boy,
each with a hand on the bridle straps.

To the girl her hat, to the boy her smile,
to the horse with practised ease she rose
and flowed upon its coat,
Bare leg, bare back
the horse and her as one.

The children turning, watching
the circle of the riding,
and the watching wore the colours of the meadow,
and the riding wore the colours of the sky.

Full Moon

See her as she glides the sky
Lighting the earth, lightening me
Incumbent in this dreary night.
Dark and silver her enchantment
Dark and silver in the gloom
She sees my weary footsteps safe.
And now she dons some woolly cloud
A mantle: warmth and privacy.
Has she sought and found her lover
Striding in her magic light,
Or was he in a cave interred
In slumber? She beside his bed
With gentle kisses for his eyes
And so he sleeps forever young.

Feeding Time

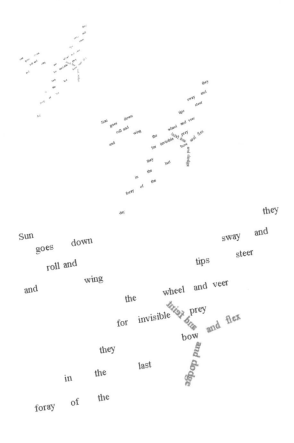

Sun goes down
roll and
and wing

they
sway and
tips steer
the wheel and veer
for invisible prey
bow and flex
and teeter
and dodge
they
in the last
foray of the

day

Heaving Ground Elder

The ground-elder is rife this year,
lush green and pumped up from the rain.
Its white umbels our umbrage,
fuelling our obsessions and piled up grievances
to chip mugs, or throw plates.
Time to leave room leave house,
vacate our space and remember when ground-elder
could be vanquished. Now, creative clutter,
pastime inventory is as pointless
waste of space and makes us choose
between sifting soil or breaking new ground.

Dorothy Marion Langrish

1912 – 2007. Teacher extraordinaire. Every one was a child to
Aunty Do.

Dorothy Marion you've gone away,
Gone to the place that was always your own.
Did you wake with a smile when He called out your
                                                      name,
Did you rise like the dawn and its chorus?

Did you pack a small bag with the poems you love
And with memories of loved ones and places you've
                                                      been,
Did you go with light footfalls, a skip in your step
Leaving behind old age and decline?

Did you watch for the children whose minds you
                                          have touched
Who you've nourished with wisdom, who'll always
                                                love you,
Did you share in their loss at the time of your going,
Did your gain give them joy in their mourning?

Did they come to collect you with kindness and
                                                  kisses,
Did your friend come to greet you, to carry you
                                                  home,
Did the air ring with tears and with laughter,
Did they make you a flower of the Garden?

Privacy

The ones in mind know about illusion,
about silent speeches glossed with mood.
They take liberty to wander into daydream
detached from sense in privacy.

But particularly concerned with how the body looks
and cautiously attached to mouth and ear
they speak carefully, listen patiently
ready to digress, divert or misdirect.

And one, attached to sense and reflex
intrudes, and feels heads turn,
and eyes and silent questions tear
at clothes, and one assaulted and exposed retreats.

Waspish

She came before daylight, dancing on air,
summoned by the kitchen's glare,
drawn by a warmth in dressing gown
where wisps and curls of sleep were steaming.
While I was stirring sugar into tea
she was tapping on the window pane,
I hardly noticed her at all.

So woe was me when I opened the door!

We hovered eye to eye and saw alarm.
In me a crinkling diffidence,
in her a buzzy cold belligerence.
She flew up to be preoccupied
with badgering the ceiling light,
I flew down to rummage in a cupboard
and rose, insecticide in hand and mind.

Firework

Over the rooftop coming your way
with the cree of the screech
of an unoiled wheel,
the cut and the chase
of children at play
and a dash of a firework's
burst and spray.
Here

we

come!

Once Upon an Ordinary Girl

(Myra Hindley, End of Days: 36 years in prison for her part in
the Moors Murders, where she died, aged 60)

At sunrise a routine of locks and food and exercise,
of endless, relentless recurrence,
she like a child among   children
          watched,   tended,   organised.

Her wages these:
     derision of aspiration,   disbelief of motive,
                                        discount of worth
and others' passion roused to anger.

What images, what black thoughts in the night?
She made these and remembers
     for her conscience   or others' appeasement
the wilderness of the moor.
Each tragedy interred
after
               painful   screaming
     terror,

                                        and death.
Each bringing   each night
bewilderment into the dark,

And trails of devastation
of wailing mothers, crumbled children,
          For these,
                              no atonement.

Interned for longer than her   dreary life
not knowing if she could,
                                    if she would
change it for another,

When each night the light turned out
towards her future, hell's burning fire's shone.

Those who peddle the cycles of   Evil,
                                        meaning   maleficence
Those who throw the stones of accusation,
                                              meaning   guilt
Those who hawk the bile of revulsion,
                                    meaning   hatred,

Are reduced by a death
And a lost soul with nowhere to go.

For this one, who had sixty years and no tomorrow
The challenge of redemption dead,
              Interred in dull   clay   to rest

                        in oblivion.

October Moon

When nights are longer than the day,
dark seasons.
The time to which she lends her name
begins with a dark half – dark first.
She rises after noon, high in the sky
when the sun goes down,
ending the bright time
at the night time
and so begins a day,

dark days in dark seasons,

darkness favouring her face
dark as the world under, beyond the sea,
in darkness birth and death.

In dark months descending from the north
where twilight is longest
where dead souls wait,
see the cauldron that poets seek.
Nine damsels warm it with their breath
while tending piglets.
With darkness growing in her face
she seeks the sun.

Then see her as barge
and cargo of soul
bound for the dawn.
~

Dark moon rising – I can't see you
but I know you're there

Dark of moon and bats twitter,
 the Wild Hunter, once white,
ranges the sky with ghostly raucous hounds
gathers the souls of the dead
to himself, to the world under.

See her anew, grown of flowers
in the south, in summer lands
born after sunrise, already youthful.
Impetuous, leaping from mountains,
her silver bow strung, and silver arrows
for hearts of fawns and men
she skips behind the sun till nightfall

but at night an owl, white and wise.
About her in her silent flight
between her stations.
Smell the carrion she devours.

Bright days –

see her full bellied,
Mother with Child
rising in the night.
Then see her flower faced
light - white on dark night
Mother of fruit, of fruitful things
At whose behest corn grows,
children born, reborn, grow.
We sing, we dance, we honour her, us

made youthful, strong in silver light.
~

Northward bound where the dead souls wait,
see her high in the sky at sunrise
darkness growing in her face

dark days.

Dead or Alive

... a superposition of a dead and a living cat...

"I don't like it, and I'm sorry I ever had anything to do with it." Erwin Schrödinger 1887 – 1961

On that grey asphalt under that night
packets of steel were scooting and straining
to and fro where a cat crossed

and engaged with a wheel and its weight.
I saw, from inside my steel, I heard yowl
of risk realised and bones' snap

so I stopped at the roadside to mourn
but the cat raised its head with the power of suns,
with soul on fire and eyes black.

Then its forelegs swam on the tar,
paddles hauling the carnage to the bank,
to the hedge, and beyond awe.

The Dark That Can't Be Seen

Halloween 2006

Between the shadow and the shade
is the Dark that can't be seen
and eyes' fires rest
on patches of black
devoid of detail.

Behind the closed door
the Dark that can't be seen
is thriving in private,
and cats stalk
rats that lash pink tails
and no chink
lets in the light.

In the night
the Dark that can't be seen
vies with faint light
for eye's sensation,
and malicious spectres imagined
between bed and bathroom,
where feet unseen
assume their steps are sure.

Under the ground
is the Dark that can't be seen.
It hears the voles scratch,
and in the grave,
inside the box with the closed lid,
when the bell has stilled
and dreams are done
it waits for worms.

Invisible

I watch, I wear a discontent
for your eyes that do not see me,
for your ears that do not hear me
or your skin feel my touch -

it penetrates, and I with more eye to see
pain and crap that floats unnoticed
but never quite sure how you are,
oblivious to me.

So I unseen resort to over-interest
in distraction, cheer, and prospect of other
good, keeping good thanks, in good cheer
wishing for your eyes' touch.

Newest moon

There are other worlds than this.

Weighty things
bullish, grasping, clutching
circling warily
tugging at oceans
forever falling
through oppressive distance in the dark.

In moments when the clouds are scarce
Regard that moon that shines
with a light not of her own.
See her at dawn, dusk –
see her darkness brighten
in Gaia's ghostly light.

With curves of glass
see her grow, and dim. Dark and dusty
faded Prima Donna,
Her face turned ever earthward
pock and outgrowth scarred
with ancient ravages of time.

Her daily way from east to west
where the sun goes
belied: her own way west to east
she falls upon the drift of stars.

The Silliest Thing

The silliest thing we ever have done
is drilling through the floor of the sea
unloading all the planet's latent energy
for something to burn.

So why does it seem like a shotgun
loaded for a thousand million years,
firing off both barrels to the open air
to get the greenhouse warm.

I'm moving again just like I always do
but I know deep down
the silliest thing that I ever do
is driving at a hundred miles an hour,

taking comfort, showing off my zippy car
with nowhere to go.
I'm flying again like I always will
but deep down I know

it's the silliest thing.

All at Sea

Sappho

Sigh and murmur tell of the loss to loves surge,
mouth at mouth and nibble at lip and tongues press,
palm at cheek with delicate touch to soft skin,
ripples on smooth sea.

Arms that wrap and binding of breast to soft breast,
hands that stroke invoking the heights of loves swell.
Eye sees eye and, ravenous, feeds the seen need
riding on loves tide.

Rock and sway and tangle of leg in tight mesh,
moist and warm, a glistening sheen on skins' cloy
Rush and rising water and break of loves wave,
Thunder and flung spume.